Six Themes
Everyone Should Know

1 and 2 Timothy

Thomas G. Long

Geneva
Press

First edition
Published by Geneva Press
Louisville, Kentucky

18 19 20 21 22 23 24 25 26 27 —10 9 8 7 6 5 4 3 2 1

Cover designer: Rebecca Kueber

Library of Congress Cataloging-in-Publication Data

Names: Long, Thomas G., 1946- author.
Title: Six themes in 1 and 2 Timothy everyone should know / Thomas G. Long.
Description: First [edition]. | Louisville, KY: Geneva Press, 2018. |
  Series: Six themes everyone should know series
Identifiers: LCCN 2018036033 (print) | LCCN 2018037105 (ebook) | ISBN
  9781611649260 (ebook) | ISBN 9781571532398 (pbk.)
Subjects: LCSH: Bible. Timothy--Theology.
Classification: LCC BS2745.52 (ebook) | LCC BS2745.52 .L66 2018 (print) | DDC
  227/.8306--dc23
LC record available at https://lccn.loc.gov/2018036033

Most Geneva Press books are available at special quantity discounts when purchased in bulk by corporations, organizations, and special-interest groups. For more information, please e-mail SpecialSales@GenevaPress.com.

Contents

Six Themes Everyone Should Know series

The Bible, by Barry Ensign-George

Genesis, by W. Eugene March

Matthew, by James E. Davison

Luke, by John T. Carroll

1 and 2 Timothy, by Thomas G. Long

Introduction to the
Six Themes Everyone Should Know series

The *Six Themes Everyone Should Know* series focuses on the study of Scripture. Bible study is vital to the lives of churches. Churches need ways of studying Scripture that can fit a variety of contexts and group needs. *Six Themes Everyone Should Know* studies offer a central feature of church adult educational programs. Their flexibility and accessibility make it possible to have short-term studies that introduce biblical books and their main themes.

Six Themes Everyone Should Know consists of six chapters that introduce major biblical themes. At the core of each chapter is an introduction and three major sections. These sections relate to key dimensions of Bible study. These sections ask:

- What does this biblical theme mean?
- What is the meaning of this biblical theme for the life of faith?
- What does this biblical theme mean for the church at this point in history for action?

This format presents a compact and accessible way for people in various educational settings to gain knowledge about major themes in the biblical books; to experience the impact of what Scripture means for Christian devotion to God; and to consider ways Scripture can lead to new directions for the church in action.

Introduction to *1 and 2 Timothy*

The books of 1 and 2 Timothy, tucked away near the end of the New Testament along with Titus, are called the "Pastoral Epistles." They have been seen as letters written by Paul—or, today, most scholars believe, a "pastor" who writes in Paul's name and continued Paul's views—to encourage and strengthen churches that were seeking around the end of the first century to establish order, discipline, and theological fidelity.

Yet, the two letters to Timothy are not highly used by Christians and not frequently preached on by pastors. They address issues of controversy and difficulty in early congregations. These folks were trying to institute ways of ordering church life so they could live the lives to which they were called by Jesus Christ: "Do good, to be rich in good works, generous, and ready to share" (1 Timothy 6:18). They are told that through all church squabbles and disagreements, faithfulness to the gospel should be primary so Christians "may take hold of the life that really is life" (6:19).

The six themes explored here enable us in the church today to hear the gospel as expressed to these early Christians. We need to concentrate on worship, be led by faithful leaders, stay strong in the faith, love God more than wealth, hear and live God's Word, and serve faithfully in the church. These themes can strengthen our lives of faith as well as the church's witness and service to Jesus Christ.

The last words of 1 Timothy are a blessing for us as well: "Grace be with you" (6:21).

Biblical Backgrounds to 1 and 2 Timothy

Author and Date

"Although some New Testament scholars think that 1 Timothy was written by the actual apostle Paul, and probably near the end of his life, most scholars take a different position. They see this letter as written by an unknown author and as coming from late in the first century, probably after Paul was dead (which is the position taken in this [study]). So this is the signature not of the historical Paul the apostle but a literary 'Paul.'"

—Thomas G. Long, *1 & 2 Timothy and Titus*. Belief: A Theological Commentary on the Bible (Louisville, KY: Westminster John Knox Press, 2016), 20.

Major Concerns

"The Pastoral Letters belong to the postapostolic age and are addressed to the concerns of second-generation Christianity. No longer were Christians convinced that the world-order would soon pass away with the glorious return of the Christ. The spiritual vigor that characterized the Pauline missions was replaced by an equally serious mandate: to establish the church as 'the pillar and bulwark of the truth' (1 Tim. 3:15)."

—James L. Price Jr., "Timothy, the First and Second Letters of Paul to, and Titus, the Letter of Paul to," in *Harper's Bible Dictionary*, ed. Paul J. Achtemeier (San Francisco: Harper & Row, Publishers, 1985), 1075.

Importance

"To read these documents as Scripture does mean recognizing that the church has included them in the canon of Scripture because, through the centuries, it has heard gospel in them and found its life formed by them more fully into the pattern of Jesus Christ."

—Long, *1 & 2 Timothy and Titus*, 8.

*Worship is not one of the activities of the church;
it is the central activity of the church.*

Chapter 1

Worship at the Center of the Christian Life

Scripture
1 Timothy 2:1–15   A church in the middle of strife and conflict is reminded that worship is central to the life of the Christian faith and that a congregation vital and faithful in worship will be healthy in the rest of its life.

Prayer
O God, you are the center of our life and the One whom we adore. In our worship, keep us from being distracted by the baubles and bright lights of this world. In our praying, keep us focused on you, and draw together all our thoughts with the tether of your will. As we worship, let us open our hands to your presence, our minds to your teaching, and our hearts to your mercy, through Jesus Christ, who gave himself for all. Amen.

Introduction
1 Timothy is one of three brief New Testament letters known collectively as the "Pastoral Epistles" (the other two are 2 Timothy and Titus). They are called "pastoral" because they present themselves as letters written by an aging pastor, the apostle Paul, now nearing death (see 2 Timothy 4:6–9), and they are addressed to young pastors, Timothy and Titus, giving wisdom about how to conduct their ministries in the face of difficult challenges.

Today we sign letters at the end, but in the ancient world writers signed their names at the beginning of letters, and all three Pastoral Epistles are "signed" in the very first verse by Paul (1 Timothy 1:1, 2 Timothy 1:1, Titus 1:1). Even so, most biblical scholars (but not all) are persuaded that these letters were written in the name of Paul by a later writer whose identity we do not know (we will call him "the Pastor"). The pastorals were written probably in the late first or early second century, almost certainly after Paul's death. There are three main reasons to think that the pastorals postdate Paul:

The "Paul" in these letters doesn't sound quite like the Paul of Romans and Corinthians. His tone is a shade sterner, and he evidences a deeper concern for church discipline and right doctrine than does the apostle Paul.

The churches reflected in these letters seem to have developed beyond the infant Christian communities addressed by the apostle Paul. They are concerned with more developed matters such as the qualifications for bishops (see 1 Timothy 3:1–7), and "the gospel" has come to mean a fairly settled body of teaching (see 1 Timothy 1:10–11).

It is difficult to fit the places and events named in these letters neatly into what we know of the life and travels of Paul the apostle. Thus, the Pastoral Epistles were likely addressed to Christian communities in the late first or early second centuries. As is the case with most of the New Testament letters, they were probably read aloud in worship, and the original hearers of these letters surely knew that Paul was no longer around. News of Paul's death would have traveled quickly and widely in the earliest churches. So, these letters were received as answers to the question, "What would the revered apostle Paul have said about the problems that face us now?" The problem under the spotlight in the passage before us is one of the most demanding in congregational life: faithful worship.

A Basic Theme: The Centrality of Worship
The church addressed in our passage is depicted as located in Ephesus, a significant port city in what is today Turkey, and Timothy is

its pastor (1 Timothy 1:3). But the main thing to know about this church is that it was in trouble. Before 1 Timothy is done, a whole laundry list of congregational problems will have been addressed, from false teaching to bitter conflict to poor leadership, but at the top of this list is a concern about worship. This is not surprising. When there is conflict anywhere in the body of a congregation, the first symptoms usually show up in worship. When members of a congregation begin to grouse about the hymns, the sermons, or the style of the liturgy, or when bickering breaks out in the choir loft or in the worship committee, it is often the case that there is distress elsewhere in the life of the church. A struggle for power or control in the congregation can erupt as a dispute over old hymns versus contemporary music, over whether it's good to have a children's sermon, or if it's permissible to applaud in the service.

The converse is also true. Harmony in worship generally signals harmony throughout the life of the congregation. The reason for this relationship between worship and the health of congregational life is that worship is not merely one of the many activities of the church. It is the *central* act of the church, pulsating out to every other arena of the church's life.

Theologian Geoffrey Wainwright wrote, "Worship . . . is the point of concentration at which the whole of the Christian life comes to ritual focus."[1] What this means is that every aspect of being a Christian, every ministry and expression of the church, can be found in microcosm in the rituals of worship. The sermon reverberates out into the whole church's witness to the world. The Lord's Supper stands at the epicenter of all other meals—the family dinner table, the church supper in the fellowship hall, the meals served in the homeless shelter, the love and fellowship of friends gathered around a common table. The prayers for those who are ill or grieving radiate into acts of compassion at bedside and graveside. The cleansing and renewing water of baptism finds expression in all ministries of reconciliation and in every attempt to point to the image of God in all humanity.

No wonder then the Pastor of 1 Timothy, concerned about the many problems of the church pastored by young Timothy, turns

---

1. Geoffrey Wainwright, *Doxology: The Praise of God Is Worship, Doctrine, and Life: A Systematic Theology* (New York: Oxford University Press, 1980), 8.

very early to the issue of worship. Like a physician placing a stethoscope over a patient's heart, listening to the rhythm of heartbeat, the Pastor places his stethoscope over the heart of worship. When he hears an irregular heartbeat, he knows that a sickness in worship puts everything else about the life of the church at risk.

The Life of Faith: Standing in the Need of Prayer

A service of worship is essentially a long conversation between God and the worshipers. This is essential for the life of faith. Sometimes God speaks to the people, mainly in sermons and Scripture, and sometimes the people speak to God, in prayers, creeds, hymns, and ascriptions of praise. The fact that worship is a dialogue between God and the people is a sign that the whole of worship is prayer. There are specific prayers *in* the service of worship, of course, but in a larger sense the entire act of worship is prayer—speaking and listening in the context of a deep and trusting relationship with God.

First Timothy 2:1–7 is the lengthiest treatment of prayer in the New Testament.[2] The passage addresses some particular issues about praying rightly, but it soon soars into a powerful hymn about our relationship through Christ with the saving and merciful God (vv. 3–6). In other words, the details about proper prayer are nestled into the larger relationship with God that makes prayer possible.

Two specific prayer issues are addressed in this passage:

The scope of prayer. How big should we make our prayers? Very big, according to the Pastor. He urges that every kind of praying that we do—"supplications, prayers, intercessions, and thanksgivings" (v. 1)—be done for everyone, not some or a few, but *everyone*. This counsel undercuts all attempts to narrow our prayer concerns. Our tendency is to pray for our loved ones but not those far away, our nation but not others, ourselves but not our neighbors, our church but not those unlike us. Quite pointedly, there is plenty of evidence that the church addressed in this letter was in deep and acrimonious

2. Robert W. Wall with Richard B. Steele, *1 and 2 Timothy and Titus* (Grand Rapids: Wm. B. Eerdmans Publishing Co., 2012), 79.

conflict. That may be the hardest praying of all, to pray not only for yourself but also for the person in the next pew who, for a season, has become an enemy.

The scope of prayer is so large, says the Pastor, that we should pray even "for kings and all who are in high positions" (v. 2). At the time this letter was written, this was a radical and disturbing view because this meant praying for the emperor of the cruel and despotic Roman Empire. The Romans considered their Caesar to be a quasi-divine figure and demanded full devotion and obeisance from his subjects. Notice, however, that the Pastor urges the church to pray *for* the emperor, not *to* the emperor, and therein lies a world of difference. Despite his posturing, the emperor is not divine. Indeed, "there is one God; there is also one mediator between God and humankind, Christ Jesus" (v. 5).

The reason for prayer. Why pray? The Pastor suggests that the overarching reason for all prayer is hope in the saving power of God. God, says the Pastor, "desires everyone to be saved and to come to the knowledge of the truth" (v. 4), and prayer is participation in the saving and reconciling work of God. There is hope even that the violent tendencies of the emperor might be gathered into the will of God, allowing people "to live a quiet and peaceable life in all godliness and dignity" (v. 2b).

The Church: Men Behaving Badly . . . and Women, Too

We are not completely in the know about the circumstances to which 1 Timothy is addressed, but we know enough to realize that the church was in crisis. As for the men in the congregation, some of them had abandoned the truth of the gospel in favor of superficial and destructive pseudo-religious nonsense (see 1 Timothy 1:3–7). Some of them taught this fluff at the top of their lungs and in argumentative tones. Some of the women in the congregation had been victimized by this foolishness, imperiling their ability to live a Christian life (see 2 Timothy 3:1–9).

Again, the Pastor is persuaded that the place to begin correcting these problems is in worship, and he offers specific instruction to men and to women. A few years ago, a bestselling book, *Men Are from Mars, Women Are from Venus*, got a lot of mileage out of the opinion that the genders are, down deep, very different temperamentally. This idea, that men and women are essentially very different creatures, was also the predominant understanding of the ancient world, an outlook shared by the Pastor of 1 Timothy. For him, men have hot blood running in their veins and are prone to violence, while women are the weaker sex, easily swayed by emotion. Thus, he counsels men should pray "lifting up holy hands without anger or argument" (1 Timothy 2:8b), and he advises women to "learn in silence, with full submission" (2:11b).

Today we raise an eyebrow of suspicion over the idea of fixed male and female roles and temperaments. But we do not have to share the Pastor's views of gender, and certainly not the assumptions of a patriarchal society about the need for women to submit to supposed male superiority, to hear the wisdom about worship offered in this passage, about the importance of faithful worship in the midst of church conflict. There are three items of wise counsel:

> *The posture of prayer: hands open and lifted (2:8).* Here the human body expresses a receptivity to God and a confession of dependence on God's grace. A Christian who stands in worship with hands outstretched in surrender to God's mercy is unlikely to turn toward a fellow worshiper with clinched fists.

> *Dress in worship.* The Pastor's instruction is not to come to worship with "hair braided, or with gold, pearls, or expensive clothes" (2:9b). Some commentators think the Pastor is alarmed that some women were coming to worship trying to look sexually alluring. But Latin American biblical scholar Elsa Támez is probably closer to the truth when she thinks the issue was about class. These folks in Timothy's church were not trying to look sexy—they were trying to look *rich*, thus vaunting themselves over their poorer fellow worshipers.

> *"Learn in silence" (2:11).* Although the Pastor here addresses women in worship, we can discover an insight for all worshipers. New Testament scholar Luke Timothy Johnson translates

this phrase "to be in the quiet as you learn,"[3] a reminder that the proper attitude for every worshiper is humble receptivity.

For Reflection and Action

1. In the study, the statement is made, "When there is conflict anywhere in the body of a congregation, the first symptoms usually show up in worship." Do you agree? Why or why not?

2. The author of 1 Timothy urges the church to pray "for kings and all who are in high positions" (2:2). In our own time, this would mean praying for presidents, governors, members of Congress, and so forth, even if we did not support these people politically. Why do you think the church should pray for such civic leaders?

3. One of the issues that the author of 1 Timothy addresses is the matter of proper dress in worship. Obviously, dress codes and standards change over time. What do you think is wise counsel about dress in worship today?

3. Luke Timothy Johnson, *The First and Second Letters to Timothy* (New York: Doubleday, 2001), 201.

Scripture offers us a look at first-century descriptions of church leaders to see the underlying and enduring qualities that make for good leaders in the church.

Chapter 2

The Importance of Faithful Leadership

Scripture
1 Timothy 3:1–13; 5:17–22   In both of these passages, the writer of 1 Timothy addresses the desired virtues of good leaders in the church and warns about what may happen when leaders lose their bearings.

Prayer
O God, who appointed Moses and Aaron as leaders of the people of Israel, give to your church leaders deep faith, great courage, and profound wisdom. Through them, guide your church beside the still waters, in the paths of righteousness, and even through the valley of the shadow, bringing us at last to the land of promise and peace. In the name of the Great Shepherd, even Jesus Christ, our Lord. Amen.

Introduction
In these two passages in 1 Timothy (and a similar one in Titus 1:5–9), the Pastor describes the desired qualities for leaders in the church. No one writes essays on leadership in a vacuum, but only in response to real problems on the ground. Indeed, some of the leaders in this community have clearly gone off the rails, and the causes form a sad and familiar litany—ego, money, and sex. Some of the congregational leaders, charged with being teachers, unfortunately became swollen with pride and began to teach their own brand

of religious nonsense instead of the gospel (1 Timothy 1:3–7), some were tempted by greed (1 Timothy 6:2b–10), and whispers of sexual impropriety were in the air (1 Timothy 5:2b). Here the Pastor tries to refresh the church's memory of what true leadership is all about.

Congregations in the late first and early second centuries usually consisted of clusters of house churches. Christians, for the most part, worshiped in small groups in private homes, groups often composed of the family members and household servants who lived and worked in the home (see, for example, Romans 16:3–5b). Each house church had a leader, called both "elder" and "bishop." In the same way that today's clergy have several titles—pastor, priest, rector, preacher, and so forth—to reflect the several dimensions of ministry, house church leaders were called "elder" to reflect their teaching, preaching, and worship leadership roles, and also "bishop" to reflect their guidance and governance roles. These elders/bishops had assistants, known as deacons (the word means "servant"), who carried out the practical work of caring for widows and orphans and other ministries of compassion.

Eventually, as Christian communities grew in size and complexity, the title "bishop" (the word means "overseer") began to describe a separate leadership role, namely the person who served in a community as the supervisor over the elders in charge of the various house churches. Thus, there gradually developed a three-tiered structure of leadership: bishop, elder, and deacon. Although our historical knowledge of church organization in this period is sketchy, it is likely that in the time of 1 Timothy the church still had only a two-tiered leadership structure: elder/bishop and deacon.

A Basic Theme: A Christian Leader's Job Description

What qualities should the church seek in its leaders? The answer to this question can easily become confused, because sometimes congregations are so desperate to fill leadership slots, they are ready to take anyone who shows up willing to work, regardless of character or temperament. On other occasions, churches set utterly secular standards for their spiritual leaders. One minister, who was being considered for a call by a pastor nominating committee, read the position description and thought, "This is a corporate model. They want a CEO, not a pastor."

In 1 Timothy 3:1–8, the Pastor tackles this thorny issue, mainly because the leadership in the church he addresses is in disarray. Poor leaders have damaged the life of this congregation, and the Pastor believes the church needs to return to basics. He describes the list of qualities desired in a "bishop," which, in the early church was a role much like our "pastor" or "elder."

We need to look at this passage's underlying vision of leadership rather than simply at the surface items on the list, which sometimes express values rooted more in the first-century world than in ours. For example, the demand that a bishop "keep his children submissive and respectful in every way" (v. 4) reflects the far more restrictive parenting conditions of the ancient world. A child today who goes through a phase of adolescent rebellion is not necessarily the result of neglectful parenting. Likewise, saying that an elder should be "the husband of one wife" (v. 2, KJV), actually points to the deeper quality of steadfastness, but this verse unfortunately led one very devout layman to refuse to serve as an elder because he was single!

The desired qualities for a bishop fall into three areas: temperament, reliability, and skill. In terms of temperament, such qualities are named as being hospitable, gentle in spirit, not a lover of money, and highly regarded among outsiders. Because the gospel is welcoming to all, so must be the leaders. Because the gospel is offered without price, so leaders should not desire personal profit. Because the gospel is a word of peace and reconciliation to the world, so should the leaders be people of peace and well-esteemed even by outsiders.

Several items in the Pastor's list of virtues point to the issue of reliability. Being "above reproach" and steadfast in marriage are expressions of the deeper truth that a person can be counted on and trusted in close relationships. The Pastor steers the church away from turning new converts into bishops. It's not that the Pastor doubts the authenticity of anyone's conversion, but rather that it takes time to determine whether the first flowering of faith has taken deep root.

Finally, a leader needs to show the skills of good teaching and stewardship of their own households. If they are ineffective teachers, how will the church grow in the gospel? If they are poor stewards of their own household resources, asks the Pastor, how can they "take care of God's church" (v. 5b)?

The Life of Faith: Ministers of Compassion

In 1 Timothy 3:8–13, the Pastor turns his attention to the qualifications for a deacon. From the earliest days of the Christian movement, churches maintained ministries of compassion to those in need, such as caring for widows (1 Timothy 5:3–16; Acts 6:1–6) and orphans (James 1:27). Because those who were bishops and elders had their hands full teaching and preaching the gospel and managing congregational life, deacons were appointed as assistants to carry out the practical duties of these ministries of compassion.

Some of the leadership qualities sought in deacons are not surprising. Obviously, the church does not want people who are "greedy for money" to be managing the benevolence budget, and overindulging in wine is a clear impediment to effective ministry (v. 8). But there are a couple of deacons' virtues that require some explanation:

The Pastor says they should be "serious" and "not double-tongued" (v. 8). As we might say it today, they should not talk out of both sides of their mouths. The reason for this is that the deacons, as they performed their ministries, were engaged in regular, perhaps daily, contact with people in the congregation. In a time before e-mails, and even newsletters, the deacons were the communication network of the church, and a gossipy deacon, or one who flattered people to their faces but criticized them behind their backs, could do enormous damage to the gospel. It was important, then, for deacons to guard their tongues. The gospel depends upon truthful speech and honest, transparent relationships, and loose talk and idle gossip undermined that integrity.

The deacon "must hold fast to the mystery of the faith with a clear conscience" (v. 9). The "mystery of the faith" is shorthand for the whole truth and meaning of Jesus Christ (see the summary of the mystery in v. 16). The reason for this is that deacons are more than just "do-gooders." Their ministry is an expression of the gospel, and it is also difficult, demanding, and sometimes discouraging work. Only a ministry of compassion that is planted deeply in faith can avoid evaporating in the fires of resistance or fading away under the hot sun of setbacks and discouragements. This is why deacons should be trained and job-tested (v. 10). This test is not only about skill and character, but about endurance nourished by Christian hope, a hope that gives "great boldness in the faith that is in Christ Jesus" (v. 13b).

The Greek word *gynaikas* in 1 Timothy 3:11 can be translated two ways. It can mean *"wives,"* that is, the wives of deacons. More likely, however, it means *"women,"* that is, women who *are* deacons, an indication that even in these earliest days of the church women were in significant positions of leadership (see Romans 16:1). The same qualities expected of male deacons—seriousness of speech, a temperate spirit, and deep faith (1 Timothy 3:11)—are also sought in women who serve in this ministry.

Like these deacons, all of us can be ministers of compassion in our lives of faith.

The Church: Leadership in Practice . . .
What Could Go Wrong?

In 1 Timothy 3, the Pastor named qualities desired in leaders. That was the game plan; now, in chapter 5, the Pastor describes what has actually been happening on the field. Leadership on paper is one thing, but leadership in action is quite another, and problems had erupted in the church. In the Watergate movie *All the President's Men*, one of the characters utters an iconic line: "Follow the money." The Pastor would have agreed. Later he will write "the love of money is a root of all kinds of evil" (1 Timothy 6:10). The leadership problems were tangled, but the way to unsnarl them was to "follow the money."

Each house church had a leader—a bishop/elder—who served as teacher, preacher, worship leader, and guide. These tasks demanded a lot of effort, and the house church contributed money so the bishops/elders could receive stipends for their labor. The problem was that some of the leaders had figured out that if they taught what people wanted to hear rather than the gospel they truly needed, the stipends got fatter. In another letter, the Pastor warned about this. People have "itching ears" for false teaching, he said, so, "they will accumulate for themselves teachers to suit their own desires" (2 Timothy 4:3).

The gospel is good news, but it is demanding good news. It summons every aspect of life into obedience to Christ. Dietrich Bonhoeffer once said that when Christ calls us, he bids us to "come and die."[1] There has always been a market for teaching and preaching that sounds vaguely like the gospel but is sweeter, easier, more self-flattering, and less challenging than the real thing. Some of the elders in the church of 1 Timothy had discovered that "itching ears" for smooth teaching leads to full collection plates.

It might seem like the way out would be to cut off stipends altogether and to make leadership a completely volunteer activity. But the Pastor advises a different path. He quotes Jesus, "The laborer deserves to be paid" (see Luke 10:7) and says good leaders are "worthy of double honor" (probably the honor of respect and the honor of compensation). The task, then, is to figure out which of the leaders are teaching truthfully and ruling well (v. 17).

The Pastor knows that sifting good leaders from bad will require a difficult discernment process. The community will need to gather evidence to affirm sound leadership and rebuke the greedy false teachers. Don't let this be done through gossip or by people who bear grudges, he says. Do "nothing on the basis of partiality" and let the whole process be in the sunshine. Choosing good leaders and disciplining bad leaders is not about winning a church fight. It is the constant discernment of the church performed in the highest court of all: the presence of God, Christ, and the angels (v. 21).

For Reflection and Action

1. Suppose a friend of yours, who attends another church, is serving on the pastoral search committee to find a new minister. Your friend asks you, "What do you think is the most important quality we should desire in a new pastor?" How would you respond?

---

1. Dietrich Bonhoeffer, *The Cost of Discipleship,* trans. R. H. Fuller (New York: Touchstone, 1995), 89.

2. The study mentioned a minister who looked over a congregation's position description for pastor and said, "This is a corporate model. They want a CEO, not a pastor." What do you think this minister meant by this comment? Why do you think this minister was concerned?

3. The study says that choosing good leaders for the church requires "a difficult discernment process." What do you think are some of the ways that the church can exercise that kind of discernment?

Faith will grow weaker, unless the faithful engage in practices intended to keep faith strong.

Chapter 3

Staying Strong in the Faith

Scripture
1 Timothy 4:1-10; 2 Timothy 1:3-15; 2 Timothy 2:1-7   In all three of these passages, the Pastor gives counsel about how to keep faith strong and vital in times when it is in danger of weakening.

Prayer
O God, you have promised those who wait on you that you will renew our strength and that we will mount up with wings as eagles. Teach us, then, how to wait and trust in your Spirit, so that we can run and not be weary, walk and not faint. Through Jesus Christ, our Lord. Amen.

Introduction
1 and 2 Timothy present themselves as letters written to a young pastor, Timothy, who is struggling to lead a church in trouble. The woes of his congregation are many, but in one sense they boil down to a single problem: weakening faith. When the Christian faith was a new and fresh experience, the believers were zealous, eager to show in their lives "the faith and love that are in Christ Jesus" (1 Timothy 1:14). But faith is difficult to maintain over the long haul. The British theologian R. E. C. Browne once warned that there comes a point for every minister (indeed, every Christian) when the gospel he or she once cherished now seems too little to

17

go on. A fatigue sets in, or even, says Browne, "an atheistic anxiety," and we begin to seek lifestyles and ways of seeing the world that seem to supply more meaning and power than does the gospel.[1]

In Timothy's church, there were several symptoms of weakening faith. People no longer had an appetite for sound theology but instead had "itching ears" for teachers and teaching that suited their own desires (2 Timothy 4:3). Congregational life was marked by gossip and contention, and the love of pleasure was edging out the love of God. But this happens in every culture and time. Matthew Arnold's poem "Dover Beach," composed in the middle of the nineteenth century, described the lessening of faith the poet observed in his own time. The poem begins with a description of the sea at full tide beneath England's White Cliffs of Dover, and then the poet says:

> The Sea of Faith
> Was once, too, at the full, and round earth's shore
> Lay like the folds of a bright girdle furled.
> But now I only hear
> Its melancholy, long, withdrawing roar.[2]

Across history there have been ages of faith and ages of doubt. How does one respond in a time when faith seems to be slipping away? The Pastor who composed 1 and 2 Timothy is careful to underscore several resources, both in terms of personal discipline and congregational life, for keeping faith strong.

A Basic Theme: God's Gymnasium

In 1 Timothy 4:1–10, the Pastor who wrote the letter is concerned about how bad teaching (the "teaching of demons" he dramatically puts it—v. 1) can undermine faith. In some ways this text is difficult for us to understand because of the very different way that many in our day think about "teaching" and "doctrine." Today "doctrine" is often thought of as ideas about God that are worthy of debate. So when the Apostles' Creed invites us to confess "I believe in the holy catholic church," we often say to ourselves,

---

1. R. E. C. Browne, *The Ministry of the Word* (London: SCM Press, 1958), 40.
2. Matthew Arnold, "Dover Beach" at https://www.shmoop.com/dover-beach/poem -text.html.

"So what do I think about the church? Do I think it's holy? Do I think it's catholic, or not? Do I really believe in the holy catholic church?"

This is not the way the earliest Christians thought of teaching and doctrine. Doctrines weren't opinions to be debated but expressions of wisdom that opened up ways of seeing, trusting, and living. Doctrines were like navigational beacons in a churning and dangerous channel—guides to staying alive.

The Pastor was alarmed because false teachers in the congregation were sneaking out under the cover of darkness and moving the doctrinal navigational beacons. As a result, people were imperiled by their teaching. The details of their teaching are complex, but essentially they were advocating a super-spiritualized, ascetic version of Christianity. The more one avoided the messy circumstances of everyday life, the more pure one was. Marriage and sex are messy, so "they forbid marriage." Eating and drinking can introduce impurities into your body, so they "demand abstinence" from certain foods (v. 3).

The point here is not whether it's good to be a vegetarian, to be on a diet, or to choose to be single. The point, rather, is that the false teachers were teaching people to be suspicious about the goodness of creation. The Pastor reminds Timothy that "everything created by God is good, and nothing is to be rejected, provided it is received with thanksgiving" (v. 4). Again, this is not merely an idea, an opinion; it is a way of life. The Pastor is saying that life is richer and deeper, more joyous and holy, when we give thanks to God without ceasing for the goodness of the earth; for the gifts of marriage, sexuality, and children; for the mountains and the seas; for the nourishment of food and drink.

This faithful posture of giving thanks to God for the gifts of creation is not maintained easily or by accident, but only through constant practice. "Train yourself in godliness," advises the Pastor (v. 7). In Greek, the word translated "train" is *gumnase*, from which we get "gymnasium." How to keep faith strong? Go to God's gym every day and work out. This can take a number of forms, two of which are offered here:

The Lord's Supper. When the Pastor says that God's gifts are "sanctified by God's word and by prayer" (v. 5), this is almost certainly an allusion to the Lord's Supper. Part of going to God's gym is to receive regularly the Lord's Supper, to realize that Christ comes to us not just in lofty experiences but in the physical elements of bread and wine. "O taste and see that the LORD is good" (Psalm 34:8).

Giving thanks. Going to God's gym means everyday practices of giving thanks to God for the food we eat, giving thanks for the tomatoes growing in our garden, giving thanks for the refreshment of the rain. These prayers of thanksgiving, silent and spoken, are not just piety. They are workouts in God's gym, strengthening faith.

The Life of Faith: Remembering the Blessings

Another key to keeping faith strong, the Pastor tells Timothy, is to remember we did not generate our faith ourselves; it was given to us as a gift. Once, when Fred Rogers was the host of the children's program *Mister Rogers' Neighborhood*, he was asked to address an auspicious gathering of journalists. Usually the speakers for this group were high-level diplomats, significant politicians, and major literary figures, and one of the journalists confessed that, when he saw Fred Rogers listed as the speaker, he assumed they were in for a "light lunch." But when Fred Rogers began to speak, he took out his pocket watch and told the group that he was going to keep silent for one minute, and he invited everyone in the room to spend that minute remembering those people—parents, friends, teachers, coaches, pastors—who had made it possible for them to be the people they were. Before Mr. Rogers tucked away his watch, the journalist said that he could hear quiet sobbing around the room as those present remembered the people whose sacrifices and love had nurtured their lives.

Just so, the Pastor reminds Timothy of his grandmother, Lois, and his mother, Eunice, who passed the faith from generation to generation, and ultimately to Timothy himself (2 Timothy 1:5). Timothy's faith was no fleeting experience, no momentary fling with religion that evaporates in the morning light. It was planted deep and cultivated well by many hands in his life, and in ours.

This awareness leads to two practices that can sustain our faith:

Remember the saints. Remember the Loises and Eunices who have gone before us, the people in every congregation who fought the good fight and bore witness to the faith with their lives. One evening at the church where my family worshiped, we were holding the kickoff banquet for the annual stewardship efforts, and the choir was providing the entertainment. They sang several popular songs and Broadway tunes, and then they ended the program with a rousing rendition of "Give Me That Old-Time Religion." They were having fun with it, hamming it up as they swayed and sang, "It was good enough for Paul and Silas, . . . It was good enough for our mothers, . . . It was good enough for our fathers, it's good enough for me." But then they ran out of stanzas. The choir was silent for a moment, and then someone in the choir began to sing, "It was good enough for Mary Blanton," the name of a woman in the congregation who had died a few months before. The room became hushed, and then they sang other names of the saints passed on: "good enough for Bill Simmons, . . . good enough for Jim Sykes, . . . good enough for Sarah Langley." We were moved by the memories of those who had shaped our lives with their faith.

Remember peak moments in our journey of faith. In Timothy's case, the Pastor calls on him to remember his ordination: "rekindle the gift of God that is within you through the laying on of my hands" (v. 6). For others, the peak moments might be the birth of a child, a book we read, a sermon or a choral anthem we heard, a night sitting on a hillside watching the stars, or even a difficult time in our life when God nevertheless felt close and loving.

The Church: Soldiers, Athletes, and Farmers

To describe ways for us in the church to strengthen faith, the Pastor uses three very provocative images in 2 Timothy 2:1-7: the soldier, the athlete, and the farmer.

The members of the church should practice their faith like a "good soldier." A harsh image, perhaps, but the Pastor does not have violence in mind. The faithful are like soldiers, he says, when they do three things: 1) "share in suffering" (4:3); 2) avoid being distracted by "everyday affairs" (4:4a); and 3) "please the enlisting officer" (4:4b).

To share in suffering is to be willing to pick up one's cross every day (Luke 9:23). Strong faith is marked not by winning and lording it over others, but by humble service and by being willing to participate in the pain of others. In this spirit, Julian of Norwich is said to have prayed for three wounds, three forms of suffering: the wound of contrition (humble penitence); the wound of longing for God ("As a deer longs for flowing streams, so my soul longs for you, O God"—Psalm 42:1); and the wound of compassion (empathy with the suffering of others).[3]

To avoid the distractions of everyday life is to keep one's eye on the ball in regard to the mission of Christ. When the energies of the church are spent on peripheral issues and squabbles, the energy drain causes faith fatigue.

Finally, pleasing the "enlisting officer" is, of course, doing the will of Christ instead of our own. Whenever Christians try to accomplish their own agendas rather than following Christ's lead, the result is useless programs, lifeless worship, and a burdensome church life. When we take on Christ's yoke instead of our own, ironically our load is lightened, for "my yoke is easy and my burden is light" (Matthew 11:30).

The members of the church should practice their faith like an athlete who wins the trophy by competing "according to the rules" (v. 5). Careful, the Pastor is not talking about a stern, rulebound Christianity. Rather he is talking about knowing what game one is playing and having a feel for that game. Jesus talked about this in the Sermon on the Mount when he spoke of the danger of practicing religion in front of others to be seen by them. Almsgiving, for example, can be a game of being applauded by others. If so, then go ahead and play by those rules. Blow a trumpet, and let the congregation dedicate a

3. Julian of Norwich, *Showings*, trans. and intro. Edmund Colledge and James Walsh (New York: Paulist Press, 1978), 127.

plaque with your name on it. You'll get the reward you bargain for. But if you're playing the game of faith, then play by those rules. Give your offerings in secret where only God can see, and you will gain the reward that only God can give—a renewal of life and a strengthening of faith.

The members of the church should practice their faith like farmers who work in the fields and who receive the first share of the crops (v. 6). Those who work in God's field, tilling the gospel crops of hospitality, peacemaking, justice seeking, mercy, and sharing the good news, are the very ones who are first to be overjoyed and nourished when the great harvest arrives.

For Reflection and Action
1. Do you see signs of weakening faith in our society today? If so, where?

2. For the writer of 1 Timothy, God's "gymnasium" is the place one goes to exercise and strengthen one's faith life. It may be a Bible study, or private prayer, or serving in a soup kitchen, or a book group, or other activity. What is your faith "gymnasium" and what do you do there to strengthen your faith?

3. The writer of 2 Timothy uses three images for staying strong in the Christian faith: the soldier, the athlete, and the farmer. Which of these images is most compelling to you? Why?

A faithful and godly life comes from the worship of the true God, and rich Christians are called to "convert" from the false god of wealth to the true and living God.

Chapter 4

Wealth and the Truly Good Life

Scripture

1 Timothy 6:3-19   This passage describes the dangers of following false teachings in light of the true riches God gives while also encouraging believers to fight the good fight of faith.

Prayer

O God, our life and our hope, we live in a world consumed by the desire to acquire more and more possessions. We confess that we have often been deceived by the empty promises of wealth. Let us rest in the confidence that you alone give life, and you give it abundantly. Teach us how to be grateful for what we have, generous with those who have not, and eager to receive from your hand the life that really is life. In the name of Christ, we pray. Amen.

Introduction

A group of clergy was meeting together one day to help each other prepare for the coming Sunday's sermon. The biblical passage they were studying was the Magnificat (Luke 1:46–56), the song Mary sings after she learns she will be the mother of the Christ child. This song is a word of hope to the poor and lowly of the earth, celebrating how God has brought down the rich and powerful and lifted up the weak and needy. One of the ministers present said, "My problem is that, on Sunday, I will be preaching to the rich and powerful. What should I say to them?"

Timothy, who is depicted as the pastor of the church in Ephesus and the recipient of the letters we are studying, had the same issue. Money is always an issue in the life the church, and in so many areas. Timothy's church was no exception. We have already seen how some people in the congregation were dressing for worship in ways that said, "I'm wealthier than the rest of you" (see 1 Timothy 2:9) and how the question of paying church leaders for their service was a thorny matter (1 Timothy 5:17–18). But the more basic concern was simply the fact that some in the congregation were rich. What does the gospel have to say to them? How should they respond to the good news of Jesus Christ that fills "the hungry with good things" and sends "the rich away empty" (Luke 1:53)?

In our passage, the letter of 1 Timothy is coming to a close, and the Pastor devotes a short paragraph at the end to instructions about preaching to the rich in the congregation. In some ways, this is a bit of an add-on, an "Oh yeah, before I sign off, one more thing" statement. The endings of ancient letters were sometimes like that, miscellaneous collections of odds and ends. But in other ways, this paragraph about the rich is woven into the other material closing the letter, about sound teaching and about fighting the good fight of faith, and these two themes have much bearing on what the Pastor says about the rich.

A Basic Theme: The Love of God versus the Love of Money

The biggest problem facing Timothy's congregation, as we have already seen, is false teaching. Some leaders have replaced the solid food of the gospel with spiritual fast food, threatening the health of the congregation (see 1 Timothy 1:3–7). No surprise, then, when the Pastor returns to this theme at the end of the letter, and what he says about these teachers may sound overly harsh. They are "conceited, understanding nothing, and [have] a morbid craving for controversy and for disputes about words," he charges in 1 Timothy 6:4. This sharp attack may raise our eyebrows. Over the centuries, the church has had a sad history of trying to purify itself by rooting out heretics, and sometimes "heretics" are defined simply as people who happen to disagree with those currently in charge. Is the Pastor muscling his authority and leading the torch-and-pitchfork charge against his opponents? No, he has a more profound motive, which we can see when we note three things:

The Pastor is not speaking abstractly, as a philosopher. He is a Pastor speaking to an emergency in the life of the church. The novelist Walker Percy once imagined a convention of scholars meeting in Aspen, presenting papers. A fire breaks out in the auditorium, and a man runs to the podium shouting, "Come! I know the way out!" Everyone in the room, said Percy, would recognize the difference between the scholarly papers and this urgent announcement. The first is information that can be debated. The second is *news*. It cannot be verified in the moment, but everyone who hears it would recognize its life or death urgency.[1]

Just so, the church is in danger of wandering away from the faith, and the Pastor is crying, "I know the way out." Unfortunately, two competing voices are shouting—the false teachers, pointing one way, and the Pastor, pointing in another. So, the Pastor warns, "Don't follow that other voice!" It's not a matter of winning a power struggle; it's a matter of pointing toward life and away from danger.

The Pastor is not arguing for his own ideas but is, rather, pointing toward "the sound words of our Lord Jesus Christ" (v. 3). These "sound words" are not abstract precepts but Jesus' whole way of life. When Jesus said, "Follow me," he beckoned us to walk in his path, and the longer we follow, the deeper the holy wisdom we gain. That is why the Pastor calls Jesus' teaching "in accordance with godliness" (v. 3). Godliness is the mark of a life ever-growing into God's will, not the ability to make A's on a religion exam.

Following Jesus leads to contentment (v. 6). The more one finds peace and value in the gospel—and here is where wealth comes in—the less need there is for external validations of wealth and status. One can say, "I have enough; I am blessed." But the

1. Walker Percy, *The Message in the Bottle* (New York: Picador, 2000), 138.

false teachers have discovered that there is a financial market for bad religion, and they have an "eagerness to be rich." The result? They wander from the faith, people follow them instead of Christ, and even they are injured with self-inflicted wounds ("pierced themselves with many pains"—v. 10).

The Life of Faith: Fighting the Good Fight

A small, church-related college once had an annual award given to the student who most embodied Micah 6:8, that is, "who most does justice, loves mercy, and walks humbly with his God." The college finally abandoned the award because the recipients would be teased so relentlessly by the other students. Who in the world lives up to such perfection?

There is a bit of that feeling in 1 Timothy 6:11–16 when the Pastor urges young Timothy to walk a path of holiness in sharp contrast to the money-hungry false teachers. He calls Timothy a "man of God" and calls him to pursue "righteousness, godliness, faith, love, endurance, gentleness" (v. 11). That's a tall order, and what human being is up to such lofty goals?

The answer is that no human being can, without blemish, express all of these virtues, or, more accurately, only one human being ever perfectly embodied them: Jesus Christ. The Pastor is not urging Timothy to attempt to be righteous in his own strength, to win an ethical merit badge, but to entrust his ministry to the power of God in Christ. This is the essential meaning of the phrase to "take hold of the eternal life, to which you were called and for which you made the good confession in the presence of many witnesses" (v. 12). This alludes to Timothy's ordination—and to the baptism of all Christians—in which one's life and vocation are gathered up into Christ. So, what the Pastor is doing is not calling on Timothy to be holier-than-thou, but to keep his eye on the ball in his ministry. Your calling, the Pastor reminds Timothy, is to express the righteousness, godliness, faith, love, endurance, and gentleness of Christ, and not to pursue your own desires and interests as the false teachers do.

It is important to underscore the truth that this call to Timothy is not restricted to the clergy. Whether one is a druggist, teacher, sales manager, plumber, police officer, homemaker, banker, or other profession, the ultimate purpose of a Christian life is not to gain status, earn wealth, or accrue power, but to be a person of God and to do what one can to embody Christ's life in the world. None of us does this perfectly, but we are called to walk this path of faith, trusting God.

In our lives of faith, traveling this path will not be easy. That is why the Pastor uses battle language: "Fight the good fight of the faith" (v. 12; see also 2 Timothy 4:6–8). Traveling this path was not easy for Jesus, either. That is why the Pastor reminds Timothy of Jesus' trial before Pilate (v. 13). Jesus went through fire and fury, but he endured, and his whole life was a "good confession" (v. 13). Just so, Christians can expect resistance, temptation, scorn, and rejection, but when all is said and done, the path blazed by Christ will be shown, in his "unapproachable light" (v. 16), to be the way of life.

The Church: Life in God Is True Riches

Finally, in 1 Timothy 6:17–19, the Pastor turns to the elephant in the room: rich Christians in the congregation. This is a particularly urgent question in the churches of our day. In the early Christian congregations, there would probably have been very few rich Christians among them, but in the churches of North America almost all of us are rich. Most of us may not feel rich, but if we look at ourselves in relation to the vast population of the earth, even those of us with only modest means are near the top of the economic pyramid.

Ronald J. Sider, in *Rich Christians in an Age of Hunger,* points out how thoroughly consumerism has saturated our culture and how bombarded we are by advertising that has its own perverse "gospel," namely, that more and more acquisitions can give our lives joy, contentment, and meaning. Alluding to the Islamic confession, "There is no God but God and Muhammad is his prophet," Sider says, "Affluence is the God of twenty-first century North Americans, and the adman is his prophet."[2] "As a result," Sider goes on to say, "we are caught in an absurd materialistic spiral. The more we make, the more we think we need. . . . Somehow we need to break this cycle because it makes us sin against our needy brothers and sisters."[3]

---

2. Ronald J. Sider, *Rich Christians in an Age of Hunger* (Nashville: Thomas Nelson, 2005), 185.
3. Ibid., 186.

The Pastor tells Timothy to teach and to preach to the rich in the congregation. At first, it may appear that what Timothy is to tell the rich is a fairly mild admonition: "OK, you're wealthy, but don't keep it all for yourself. Share with those less fortunate." But the Pastor's counsel is much more radical: the rich among us need to have a conversion experience. Instead of setting their hopes on "the uncertainty of riches," they are to turn to God, "who richly provides us with everything for our enjoyment" (v. 17).

Charitable giving is, of course, a good thing. Hospitals, art museums, schools, programs to eradicate hunger, foundations devoted to good works, and more have all been established by generous philanthropy. Generous givers in congregations have supported their churches' mission. But the Pastor is not concerned here with the financial management of wealthy Christians. He is, instead, concerned about their souls. He does not want them to say to themselves, "I have plenty in the bank, and I can spare some for charity." He wants them to put their treasure not in the Chase Bank but in the coming Kingdom of God. He doesn't want us to hear the voice of God say, as God said to the rich fool, "You spent your life storing up treasures for yourself. Fool! Tonight your life is demanded of you. Where will your wealth be now?" Jesus said, "Where your treasure is there your heart will be also" (Matthew 6:21), and the Pastor wants Timothy to tell us that, if our hearts are invested in the life of God, then we will be truly rich—"rich in good works" and rich in "the life that really is life" (vv. 18–19).

For Reflection and Action

1. In 1 Timothy 6:4, the Pastor has some strong criticisms of those who, in his view, are doing false teaching. Do you think such harsh words toward others are ever justified in the life of the church? If so, when and by whom?

2. The Pastor calls Timothy to live his life as a "man of God" and encourages Timothy, as a way to stay steady on the path of godliness, to remember his ordination and baptism. Sometimes in

worship, Christians are called to "remember your baptism and be thankful." How do you think one's baptism can serve as a support and guide in living the Christian life?

3. What do you think it means today for Christians to be converted from trusting in wealth as a source of security to trusting in God?

Our stories (faith autobiographies), the stories of other Christians, and God's story come together in Jesus Christ.

Chapter 5

God's Word in Life, Story, and Scripture

Scripture
2 Timothy 3:10–4:8   The Pastor, speaking as Paul, tells stories: the story of his own life, the story of Scripture, and the story of Timothy and his ministry. God's story and the human story become intertwined realities.

Prayer
O God, you are our life, and apart from you we can do nothing. Guide us through every valley of the shadow so that, at the end, we may confess that your strength and your love have enabled us to fight the good fight of faith and to finish the race. We pray this in the name of Jesus, who is the pioneer and the perfecter of our faith. Amen.

Introduction
In the ancient world, writers of letters signed them at the beginning. Today we sign our letters at the end—"Love, Tony" . . . "Sincerely, Melissa Smith" . . . "Your friend, Olivia." The ancient letter writers would also often signal, by the way they signed the letter, something of what the letter was about. The first letter to Timothy, for example, is signed, "Paul, an apostle of Christ Jesus by the command of God our Savior and of Christ Jesus our Hope" (1 Timothy 1:1). In these few words are compressed the writer's

identity (Paul, who is an apostle), how he got that identity (by the command of Jesus Christ), and what Jesus, his commander-in-chief does (saves us and gives hope).

As another example, scholars have marveled how the signature of the Letter to the Romans rambles on for a hundred words or so, describing everything from King David to the mission to the Gentiles. Paul names his identity by describing what now gives him an identity: the whole sweep of God's redemptive history. As biblical scholar Katherine Grieb wrote, "Paul cannot introduce himself without referencing a story. Not just any story but the story that is so central to Paul's life that is in a sense what makes him 'Paul.'"[1]

In this letter, 2 Timothy, the Pastor signs his name, "Paul, an apostle of Christ Jesus by the will of God, for the sake of the promise of life that is in Christ Jesus." Once again, there is a compressed narrative in this signature. It is as if the Pastor were saying, "The story of my life has been shaped by the will of God and aimed at the promises of Christ. God's will has been the wind in my sails, and the life offered by Christ has been the harbor toward which I have always sailed."

A Basic Theme: What You Have Seen in My Life

In 2 Timothy 3:10–13, the Pastor, writing as the apostle Paul nearing the end of his life, is concerned about his legacy. No one, on his or her deathbed, ever says, "I wish I had spent more time at the photocopy machine or gossiping about my coworkers." At the end, at the summing up of things, we want to know that our life has amounted to something of significance, that we counted. The legendary preacher Charles H. Spurgeon said of John Wesley, "When John Wesley died he left behind him two silver spoons in London, two in Bristol, a teapot, and the great Methodist church."[2]

What does the Pastor say Paul left behind as his legacy?

> *Teaching.* This is mentioned first undoubtedly because, as we have seen, the biggest problem in Timothy's church was false teaching. Paul is leaving behind a legacy of teaching that can be trusted.

1. Katherine Grieb, *The Story of Romans: A Narrative Defense of God's Righteousness* (Louisville, KY: Westminster John Knox Press, 2002), xix.
2. J. Wesley Johnson, "The Last of the Great Reformers," *Munsey's Magazine* 23, no. 6 (1900): 757, 764.

Aim in life. This can be understood as "the way I lived those teachings out in my life." It's one thing to teach great truths; it is another to put them into practice in the smaller, everyday actions that make up a life. One can teach all day long about justice for the oppressed, and then go to a restaurant and treat the waiter with contempt. The Pastor is saying that Paul talked the talk, but he also walked the walk.

My faith. Here "faith" encompasses belief, but it is a stronger and deeper concept than mere assent to doctrine. By faith, the Pastor means deep trust in Christ. Paul has, against all the odds, wagered his whole life on the promises of Jesus Christ, and as the Pastor said of him earlier in this letter, "I know the one in whom I have put my trust, and I am sure that he is able to guard until that day what I have entrusted to him" (1:12). When a person makes a business investment or places a bet on the Super Bowl, the outcome is quickly and readily known. Or, "she put money in Microsoft, and it really paid dividends." But to put one's faith in Jesus Christ is to entrust one's life in a promise that will be revealed only at the end—"until that day." In the meantime, this faith looks misguided, since it involves suffering for others and carrying a cross.

Persecutions. The stories of what happened to Paul and his companions at "Antioch, Iconium, and Lystra" (3:11) were famous stories in the earliest church. After preaching in Antioch, he was run out of town; at Iconium, he was stoned by the citizens; and at Lystra, he was dragged out of the city and left for dead (see Acts 13–14). "What persecutions I endured!" Paul says (v. 11). The gospel is the word of life, but it also proclaims death to the powers and values of the world, and the world strikes out against it.

All these things—teaching, aim in life, faith, persecutions—are a part of Paul's legacy to young Timothy and the others who followed him. In essence, Paul leaves behind the story of his life, a life gathered up into the story of Christ.

The Life of Faith: As for You, Timothy

This part of 2 Timothy addresses Timothy and his ministry; 2 Timothy 3:14–4:5 is divided into two sections. The first describes the training Timothy received as a child, and the second describes the kind of ministry, as an adult, he has been trained and called to do.

In the training section, the picture that emerges is that Timothy was raised in a home that gave much attention to Timothy's formation as a Christian. The Pastor encourages Timothy to remember both what he learned and believed and from whom he learned it (v. 14). What he learned is the core of the Christian faith, namely "salvation through faith in Jesus Christ" (v. 15b), and he learned it from his family, especially his grandmother Lois and his mother Eunice (2 Timothy 1:5).

It is hard not to contrast this picture of family Christian education with what often happens today. Notre Dame sociologist Christian Smith directed a national study of the religion of American youth, finding that most Christian youth espouse a faint version of the faith, which the researchers called "Moralistic Therapeutic Deism." Theologian Kenda Creasy Dean, commenting on Smith's findings, says this boils down to "the importance of being nice, feeling good about yourself, and saving God for emergencies."[3] Youth did not invent this watered-down faith, but picked it up from their parents and their congregations, Dean says. What youth need, she says, is a faith formation in which they model themselves after truly devoted parents, learn and practice using the language of the faith, and see that the faith calls them to a mission to others that is bigger than their own personal desires.

This is, of course, the training that Timothy received. He saw dedicated faith in his grandmother and mother. He learned the language of the faith is engagement with Scripture, which "is useful . . . for training in righteousness" (v. 16), and the goal of his Christian formation was not mere personal happiness, but instead being "equipped for every good work" (v. 17). Perhaps we find familiarities here with our own journey of faith.

3. Kenda Creasy Dean, *Almost Christian* (New York: Oxford University Press, 2010), 10.

The Church: As for Me

At the funeral of a friend, a marvelous college teacher and mentor to many, I overheard a woman say, "He taught us how to live, and now he has taught us how to die." This is precisely the way in which the Pastor presents Paul, as one who taught us how to live and now is teaching us how to die. The church today needs to hear this message.

In the first section of this study, in which we looked at 2 Timothy 3:10–13, we observed how the pattern of Paul's life—his teaching, his way of life, his faith, his mission, even his sufferings—served as a model for Timothy and for other Christians. Now, in this passage, we come to the place where Paul describes his impending death.

He uses two main images to describe his death. In the first one, he says that he is "being poured out as a libation" (2 Timothy 4:6). The Pastor probably borrowed this image from Philippians 2:17–18, where Paul says, "But even if I am being poured out as a libation over the sacrifice and the offering of your faith, I am glad and rejoice with all of you—and in the same way you also must be glad and rejoice with me." A common image in the ancient world is a cup of wine or of blood being poured on an altar as a sign of devotion to a god. For Paul, it is not wine or the blood of an animal being poured out; it his own life being poured out, poured out not only for God but also for his brothers and sisters in the faith.

Quickly the Pastor changes images, from the cup being poured out to the athletic arena. Paul was an athlete for the gospel. He was a wrestler, who struggled with his opponents, with the powers of evil, and even with his own "thorn in the flesh" (see 2 Corinthians 12:7b–10), but he "fought the good fight" (v. 7a). Suddenly Paul changes uniforms. He is no longer the wrestler, but the long-distance runner, who kept going despite the heat, thirst, and weariness, and can say at the end, "I have finished the race, I have kept the faith" (v. 7b).

Together, these two images, the cup poured out and the athlete who endured to the end, present not only Paul's life, but also his death, as a constant self-giving to God and to others on behalf of the gospel. How could he have endured so long and so well? He did so by keeping his eyes on the prize, "the crown of righteousness, which the Lord, the righteous judge, will give me on that day, and not only to me but also to all who have longed for his appearing" (v. 8). Paul knew that, while the powers of this world would try to place crowns of thorns on Jesus and on those who followed him, in the light of God's coming kingdom, those crowns would turn out to be crowns of righteousness.

For Reflection and Action

1. Can you think of examples of Christians who suffered for the faith? How have their sufferings served as examples to the rest of us in our own faith?

2. In the second section of the study, we talked about Christian Smith's and Kenda Creasy Dean's views of where American youth are in their faith. Do you agree with Smith and Dean? What kind of faith formation in youth do you think the church should strive for today?

3. Our passage depicts Paul imagining himself as an athlete for the faith: a wrestler who fought the good fight and a long-distance runner who finished the race. What image—from athletics or from some other realm of life—would you employ to describe your own life of faith?

The everyday actions of a church display its connection to the cosmic reality of Christ.

Chapter 6

The Endurance
of the Church

Scripture
2 Timothy 4:9–22 Here at the ending of the second letter to Timothy, the Pastor, writing as Paul, gives a number of instructions. At first, they seem random and miscellaneous, but when we look more closely at these verses, we see a church moving ahead in confidence and mission, even in the face of adversity.

Prayer
O God, we pray for your church. It has been the body of Christ throughout the generations. There have been many times when the church has not been faithful, but you have preserved and guided us by your grace. When the way before us is unclear, show us the right path, and when our feet hesitate because we cannot see where we are going, give us the light of your Word to steady our feet and to give us courage. In the name of the Lord of the church, Jesus Christ. Amen.

Introduction
In this passage, we come to the close of 2 Timothy, and, in the ancient world, the ending section of a letter was characteristically the place where the writer would include a variety of hopes, greetings, and miscellaneous messages. We do the same today in our letters and e-mails. "Tell your wife Susan I said hello." "Hope the

big snowstorm didn't affect you too much." "I'll let you know what the doctor says when the tests come back." "Any chance for a visit next summer?" That sort of thing.

Just so, this section of 2 Timothy is filled with small messages. When we first read them, they seem almost random—"Bring the cloak that I left with Carpus, . . . Greet Prisca and Aquila, . . . Do your best to come before winter [when travel would be difficult], . . . Eubulus sends greetings to you," and so on.

When we look more closely at these verses, however, we realize that we have dropped down from 35,000 feet and are sweeping at low level over the life of the early Christian community. We see its everyday life, we observe its squabbles and infighting, we see its people at work and at prayer, and most of all we get a sense of its trust in God and its hope for the future.

Today's church is troubled in so many ways. Some congregations are exceptions, of course, but overall the Christian church in North America is growing smaller, grayer, and poorer. Once-strong churches struggle to keep the doors open, and many young people in our society choose "none of the above" as their religion.

There is no room to be complacent in the face of these difficulties. Christians should both repent that we have coveted habits of church life that betrayed the gospel and pray that God will lead us into new and more faithful ways of service. Church leaders must work tirelessly to discern what new forms and patterns the Spirit may be weaving among us that will allow us to be more faithful.

But this passage reminds us that one thing we must never do is to think that there was some earlier Camelot when the church was pure and problem free. The struggles have been there from the beginning, but this letter reminds us that finally this is Christ's church, not ours, and that the grace of Christ will guide us in the night.

A Basic Theme: Working Together and Pulling Apart

Just reading over these last verses of 2 Timothy, one is struck with the number of people who are named. There are, in fact, sixteen names mentioned in only fourteen verses. Some of these names are known to us because they appear elsewhere in the New Testament. Demas and Luke (4:10–11), for example, were mentioned in Colossians 4:14, where Demas sends greetings and Luke is called "the beloved physician." Prisca and Aquila are the very people

Paul names in Romans 16:3 as fellow mission workers, people who, Paul says, "risked their necks for my life." Others who are named, for example "Crescens," who "has gone to Galatia" (v. 10) are new names to us, although they were probably familiar to the first readers of 2 Timothy.

This list of names provides, first of all, a "family feel." Remember, 2 Timothy was almost surely written by an anonymous person—we have called him "the Pastor" in these studies—writing in the voice of the beloved apostle Paul. The names included here are from the world of the Pauline missionary movement. There is wisdom in this. Sometimes the church can become distant and impersonal, and resources and instructions from denominational headquarters (this Bible study, for example) can often feel remote and disconnected from local realities. The church, however, is at its best when it moves from the grassroots up. Jesus Christ did not create a bureaucratic structure. He created a community of disciples, a fellowship of friends. What is the church? It is not primarily the organizational structure and hierarchy. It is, rather, Timothy and Paul, Prisca and Aquila, "Linus and Claudia and all the brothers and sisters" (v. 21).

Even so, this does not mean that the church is provincial. The sixteen names at the end of this letter represent people all across the ancient world from Ephesus to Galatia, Corinth to Rome. Jesus began to preach in rural and isolated Galilee, but even now in these earliest decades of the Christian church, the community of Christ has become a world movement. Theologically, the presence and power of Jesus is not confined to this world but is a cosmic event. As the Pharisees in John observed to each other, "You see, you can do nothing. Look, the world [literally "the cosmos"] has gone after him" (John 12:19).

So, in these names mentioned in this passage, we glimpse a church that is deeply personal—like family—and yet also spread across the world. We see a church preaching the gospel to the uttermost parts of the earth, and also remaining deeply connectional in personal ways.

Yet, not all is well. That fellow Demas, who was so cheerfully sending greetings in Colossians 4:14, had evidently fallen "in love with this present world" and abandoned Paul and the mission. Somebody by the name of Alexander the coppersmith (and every congregation has at least one!) had done his best to be disruptive and to undermine Paul and his preaching of the gospel (v. 14). So, even here, the Christian church is seen doing its work and serving Christ, but not in an environment free of conflict, disloyalty, and acrimony. The Spirit continues to guide us, even in troubled times.

The Life of Faith: The Frailty of Humans and the Faithfulness of God

Our lives of faith are led by the Spirit, even as the Pastor describes Paul as having his opponents. We don't know what it means precisely that Demas fell in love with this world or why he went to Galatia (4:10). We don't know what Alexander the coppersmith's problems were with Paul's preaching, and we can hardly imagine how painful it must have been for Paul when, at a key point in his ministry, "all deserted me" (v. 16). But we do know that failures on the part of Christians and their leaders were not uncommon.

In a letter written, probably just a few years later than 2 Timothy, to the church at Philippi (the same church addressed by the New Testament letter of Philippians), Bishop Polycarp wrote:

> I am exceedingly sorry about the actions of Valens, who used to be one of your elders. He showed himself to be so ignorant of the office which was given him. I warn you therefore that you refrain from covetousness. . . . I am just grief-stricken for him and for his wife, to whom I pray that the Lord will grant true repentance. I hope that you, too, will not hold them as enemies but restore them as frail and erring members.[1]

Probably Valens had stolen or misused some of the church's money, but we see here yet another failure on the part of a Christian leader. Notice, however, that Polycarp encourages Valens to repent and for the church to seek restoration. The case of Alexander the coppersmith is either different in circumstance, or Paul, as presented by the Pastor, is not yet ready to forgive, because he urges the congregation to beware of Alexander (vv. 14–15).

---

1. Polycarp, Philippians 11:2, in *The Apostolic Fathers*, vol. 1, *I Clement, II Clement, Ignatius, Polycarp, Didache*, trans. and ed. Bart D. Ehrman, Loeb Classical Library 24 (Cambridge, MA: Harvard University Press, 2003), 347.

If the church depended upon human strength alone for its survival, it would long ago have collapsed. But the church is finally sustained by the power of God. Note the references in this passage to that sustaining power. Paul says that, at one point, everyone deserted him, but God did not. Everyone else fell away in weakness, but "the Lord stood by me and gave me strength" (vv. 16–17). And the strength God gave to Paul was not merely to protect him personally. It was that the gospel might be preached and the mission of the church might go on, "that through me the message might be fully proclaimed and all the Gentiles might hear it" (v. 17a). Paul is confident that what God has done in the past, God will continue to do in the future. "The Lord will rescue me from every attack and save me for his heavenly kingdom" (v. 18a).

Humanly speaking, the fortunes of the church go up and down. Sometimes the pews are filled, and sometimes they are not. Sometimes the church's mission gets tangled up and compromised with the values of the wider culture, and sometimes the church sees so clearly the alternative life it is called to lead. Throughout all these vicissitudes, God remains steadfastly faithful. The letter ends with an affirmation of this sustaining power of God in the life of the church, closing with the best words a young pastor like Timothy could hear: "The Lord be with your Spirit. Grace be with you" (v. 22).

The Church: Useful Christians, Risk-Taking Christians

As we have seen, the Pastor, speaking as Paul, names a number of companions in ministry, some of whom are described as having been loyal and some of whom have not. Two of these descriptions stand out particularly: the useful and the risk takers.

Useful. Paul writes, "Get Mark and bring him with you, for he is useful in my ministry" (v. 11). This word "useful" can be taken in two ways. First, people can be useful to Paul in the surface sense of providing things he needs. He needs his cloak, and he desires some books and parchments, and it will be a useful service to him to secure those possessions (v. 13). By the way, some scholars wonder why Paul, who has already alluded to the fact that he is nearing his death (vv. 6–8), would need books and other writings, and have speculated that "books and parchments" is actually a symbolic reference to Scripture. If so, the reference is very subtle, but we can say that the Pastor certainly depicts Paul's ministry as a studious one. Paul may have traveled constantly, town to town, but his ministry was not fly-by-night. It was grounded in study, in books and other writings, surely including the Scriptures.

There is a second way in which "useful" can be taken, and it refers to a discussion that took place earlier in this letter. In 2 Timothy 2:20–21, the Pastor uses the metaphor of household utensils. Every large house, he says, has two kinds of dishes and vessels, the kind that get used every day and the special occasion dishes. We would call these the "everyday china" and the "fine china." He goes on to say that even those in the church who have been disruptive, if they repent, can become fine china. They "will become special utensils, dedicated and useful to the owner of the house, ready for every good work." This is a metaphor, of course, referring to Christians who, by virtue of dedication, humility, and repentance become "useful" in doing the holy work of Christ in and through the church.

Risk takers. If some Christians are described as "useful," the presence of Prisca and Aquila in the list of names presents a second category, the "risk takers." We don't know what Prisca and Aquila did to "risk their necks" for Paul (Romans 16:4), but they did. This is the way it is in the church. Some folks in the congregation are "useful," that is, they put one foot in front of the other every day to accomplish the mission of Christ. When there is a need for a volunteer for the family night supper or the soup kitchen, they are there. When someone needs a visit in the hospital or the grief-stricken need comfort, they are there. The "risk takers" are those who know the church must always be reforming and changing and who are the first to step forward. Some people are both, of course, but the church today needs those steady "useful" members and those courageous "risk takers" as well.

For Reflection and Action

1. One of the issues raised is the tension between the church as a "family," where we know each other, and personal relationships are paramount, and the church as a "cosmic" reality, one that transcends family, kin, and personal relationships and affirms Jesus Christ as the Lord of the whole world. Where do you see this tension at work in the church today?

2. Reflect on the statement: "If the church depended on human strength alone for its survival, it would long ago have collapsed, but the church is finally sustained by the power of God." Do you think this statement is true? If not, why not? If so, how have you seen this to be true in your experience?

3. Consider two kinds of Christians: "useful" Christians, that is, those who are steady and reliable in doing God's work in the world, and "risk taker" Christians, those who are willing to advocate change and to risk themselves in the process. Are there other kinds of Christians that you see at work in the church and the world? Name some of the types you see.

Group Gatherings

Eva Stimson

Worship at the Center of the Christian Life

Main Idea

Worship is not *one* of the activities of the church; it is the *central* activity of the church. The whole of worship is prayer, an extended conversation between God and God's people. Yet, as shown in 1 Timothy, worship is often the place in congregational life where problems are revealed. A congregation vital and faithful in worship will be healthy in the rest of its life.

Preparing to Lead

- Read and reflect on chapter 1, "Worship at the Center of the Christian Life."
- Review this plan for the group gathering and select the questions and activities that you will use.
- What other questions, issues, or themes occur to you from your reflection?

Gathering

- Provide name tags and pens as people arrive.
- Provide simple refreshments; ask volunteers to bring refreshments for the next five gatherings.
- Agree on simple ground rules and organization (for example, time to begin and end; location for gatherings; welcoming all points of view; confidentiality, and so on). Encourage participants to bring their study books and Bibles.

Opening Worship
Prayer (unison)
O God, you are the center of our life and the One whom we adore. In our worship, keep us from being distracted by the baubles and bright lights of this world. In our praying, keep us focused on you, and draw together all our thoughts with the tether of your will. As we worship, let us open our hands to your presence, our minds to your teaching, and our hearts to your mercy, through Jesus Christ, who gave himself for all. Amen.

Prayerful, Reflective Reading
- Read 1 Timothy 2:1–7 aloud.
- Invite all to reflect for a few minutes in silence.
- After reflection time, invite all to listen for a word or phrase as the passage is read again and to reflect on that word or phrase in silence.
- Read the passage a third time, asking all to offer a silent prayer following the reading.
- Invite volunteers to share the word or phrase that spoke most deeply to them.

Prayer
Loving God, hear our prayers today as we seek to follow you more faithfully:

(*spoken prayers may be offered*)

Hear us now as we pray together, saying, Our Father . . .

Conversation
- Introduce Chapter 1, "Worship at the Center of the Christian Life." Share observations, reflections, and insights.
- Review the Introduction (pp. 1–2). Share these key points:
  a. 1 and 2 Timothy (along with Titus) are known as the Pastoral Epistles, offering wisdom to young pastors Timothy and Titus about how to conduct their ministries in the face of challenges.
  b. Most scholars believe these letters were written in the name of Paul in the late first or early second century. (Go over the reasons for believing the letters postdate Paul.)

c. The letters were received as answers to the question, "What would the revered apostle Paul have said about the problems that face us now?"

- Review "A Basic Theme: The Centrality of Worship" (pp. 2–4). Write "Worship" in the center of a sheet of newsprint. Call attention to the statement: "Worship is not merely one of the many activities of the church. It is the *central* act of the church, pulsating out to every other arena of the church's life" (p. 3). Ask:

  What are some of the things included in a worship service (sermon, prayers, Lord's Supper, baptism, and so forth)? Write these on the newsprint around "Worship."

  How are these rituals reflected in other areas of the church's life and witness to the world?

  Form several groups and discuss the first question in For Reflection and Action (p. 7). Share highlights of the discussions.
- Review "The Life of Faith: Standing in the Need of Prayer" (pp. 4–5). Key points:
  a. 1 Timothy 2:1–7 is the lengthiest treatment of prayer in the New Testament.
  b. The passage addresses two specific issues: (1) the scope of prayer (Who should we pray for?), and (2) the reason for prayer (hope in the saving power of God).

  Form several groups and discuss the second question in For Reflection and Action (p. 7). Share highlights of the discussions.
- Review "The Church: Men Behaving Badly . . . and Women, Too" (pp. 5–7). Form several groups. Have each group read 1 Timothy 2:8–15 and discuss:

  What is your first reaction to this passage? What problems is the Pastor trying to address? What relevance does the passage have for the church today?

  What do you think of the idea that men and women are essentially very different creatures? How is this outlook reflected in the Pastor's instructions about worship?

What do you think is wise counsel about dress in worship today?

Share highlights of the discussions.

Conclusion
Spend a minute in silent prayer and meditation, assuming the posture of prayer—hands open and lifted—as an expression of humble receptivity to God.

Passing the Peace
The peace of Christ be with you.
    And also with you.
Amen.

The Importance of Faithful Leadership

Main Idea
The writer of 1 Timothy addresses the desired virtues of good leaders in the church and warns about what may happen when leaders lose their bearings. Beneath those first-century descriptions, we can see the underlying and enduring qualities that make for good leaders in the church today: for example, hospitality, compassion, reliability, teaching, and stewardship skills.

Preparing to Lead
- Read and reflect on chapter 2, "The Importance of Faithful Leadership."
- Review this plan for the group gathering and select the questions and activities that you will use.
- What other questions, issues, or themes occur to you from your reflection?

Gathering
- Provide simple refreshments as people arrive and name tags if still needed.

Opening Worship
Prayer (unison)
O God, who appointed Moses and Aaron as leaders of the people of Israel, give to your church leaders deep faith, great courage, and profound wisdom. Through them, guide your church beside the still waters, in the paths of righteousness, and even through the valley of the shadow, bringing us at last to the land of promise and peace. In the name of the Great Shepherd, even Jesus Christ, our Lord. Amen.

Prayerful, Reflective Reading

- Read Luke 3:1–13 aloud.
- Invite all to reflect for a few minutes in silence.
- After reflection time, invite all to listen for a word or phrase as the passage is read again and to reflect on that word or phrase in silence.
- Read the passage a third time, asking all to offer a silent prayer following the reading.
- Invite volunteers to share the word or phrase that spoke most deeply to them.

Prayer

Loving God, hear our prayers today as we seek to follow you more faithfully:

(*spoken prayers may be offered*)

Hear us now as we pray together, saying, Our Father . . .

Conversation

- Introduce chapter 2, "The Importance of Faithful Leadership." Share observations, reflections, and insights.
- Review the Introduction (pp. 9–10). Share these key points:
  a. In 1 Timothy, the Pastor describes the desired qualities for church leaders.
  b. Ego, money, and sex caused leadership problems in the early church—just as in the church today.
  c. At the time of 1 Timothy, elders/bishops and deacons led house churches. As Christian communities grew in size and complexity, there gradually developed a three-tier structure of leadership: bishop, elder, and deacon.
- Review "A Basic Theme: A Christian Leader's Job Description" (pp. 10–12). Form several groups. Have each group write a job description for a pastor, using the description of an elder/bishop in 1 Timothy 3:1–7 and background from this study. Rather than listing tasks, they should focus on qualities related to temperament, reliability, and skill. They may also find it helpful to discuss the first and second questions in For Reflection and Action (pp. 14–15). Have the groups share their job descriptions.

- Review "The Life of Faith: Ministers of Compassion" (pp. 12–13). On a sheet of newsprint write "Ministries of Compassion." Ask:

  What ministries of compassion were performed by deacons in the early church?

  What ministries of compassion are needed most today?

  What leadership qualities should a deacon possess?

  How can all church members be ministers of compassion?

- Review "The Church: Leadership in Practice . . . What Could Go Wrong?" (pp. 13–14). Key points:
  a. In the early church, and often today, the best way to get at leadership problems was to "follow the money" (read 1 Timothy 6:10).
  b. Bishops/elders of house churches received stipends for their labor. Some leaders distorted the gospel and taught what people wanted to hear in order to receive bigger stipends.
  c. Distinguishing good leaders from bad is a vital task but requires a difficult discernment process.

  Form several groups and discuss the third question in For Reflection and Action (p. 15). Ask:

  Where do you see the presence of Jesus today?

  What are the areas of greatest need?

  What actions might the Spirit be leading you and/or your faith-community to take in response to those needs?

Conclusion
Invite participants to reflect daily on the third question in For Reflection and Action (p. 15).

Passing the Peace
The peace of Christ be with you.
    And also with you.
Amen.

Staying Strong
in the Faith

Main Idea
The writer of 1 and 2 Timothy encourages practices that keep faith strong and vital in times when it is in danger of weakening. These include participating in the Lord's Supper, giving thanks for the everyday gifts of God, recognizing the people and events that made faith real for us, and—like a soldier, an athlete, and a farmer—keeping our focus on the mission of Christ and avoiding distractions.

Preparing to Lead
- Read and reflect on chapter 3, "Staying Strong in the Faith."
- Review this plan for the group session and select questions and activities that you will use.
- Gather newsprint and markers, if needed, and prepare to post newsprint sheets on a wall or bulletin board.
- What other questions, issues, or themes occur to you from your reflection?

Gathering
- Provide simple refreshments as people arrive and name tags if still needed.

Opening Worship
Prayer (unison)
O God, you have promised those who wait on you that you will renew our strength and that we will mount up with wings as eagles. Teach us, then, how to wait and trust in your Spirit, so that we can run and not be weary, walk and not faint. Through Jesus Christ, our Lord. Amen.

Prayerful, Reflective Reading

- Read 2 Timothy 1:3–14 aloud.
- Invite all to reflect for a few minutes in silence.
- After reflection time, invite all to listen for a word or phrase as the passage is read again and to reflect on that word or phrase in silence.
- Read the passage a third time, asking all to offer a silent prayer following the reading.
- Invite volunteers to share the word or phrase that spoke most deeply to them.

Prayer

Loving God, hear our prayers today as we seek to follow you more faithfully:

(*spoken prayers may be offered*)

Hear us now as we pray together, saying, Our Father . . .

Conversation

- Introduce chapter 3, "Staying Strong in the Faith." Share observations, reflections, and insights.
- Review the Introduction (pp. 17–18). Share these key points:
  a. The letters of 1 and 2 Timothy are addressed to a young pastor who is struggling to lead a church plagued by weakening faith.
  b. In Timothy's church there were several symptoms of weakening faith: loss of appetite for sound theology, gossip and contention, and love of pleasure replacing love of God.
  c. The Pastor suggests resources, both in personal discipline and congregational life, for keeping faith strong.
  Ask:

    Are we living today in an age of faith or an age of doubt? Why? Why is it hard to sustain faith over the long haul?

- Review "A Basic Theme: God's Gymnasium" (pp. 18–20). On a sheet of newsprint, write "teaching" and "doctrine." Ask:

    How would you define these words? How did the early Christians think about "teaching" and "doctrine"?

Why was the writer of 1 Timothy so alarmed about false teachers in Timothy's congregation?

Form several groups and discuss the second question in For Reflection and Action (p. 23). Have each group develop a "workout plan" for keeping faith strong, using the Scripture passages from this study for ideas. Share the plans and post them on a wall or bulletin board labeled "God's Gymnasium."

- Review "The Life of Faith: Remembering the Blessings" (pp. 20–21). Have participants spend a few moments in quiet reflection on people who have influenced their faith. Then have them think about one or more peak moments in their journey of faith. Invite them to share thoughts with another person and/or write them in the form of a prayer of thanksgiving.
- Review "The Church: Soldiers, Athletes, and Farmers" (pp. 21–23). Form three groups. Give each group a sheet of newsprint labeled "soldier," "athlete," or "farmer." Have each group discuss how its assigned image suggests ways to strengthen faith. They may consider how the image is used in 2 Timothy, in other Scripture passages they may recall, and their own imagination. They may want to draw an outline of a human form on the newsprint and list ideas inside. Share the lists and post them with the workout plans in "God's Gymnasium."

Conclusion
Invite participants to share prayers of thanksgiving for those who have influenced their faith.

Passing the Peace
The peace of Christ be with you.
    And also with you.
Amen.

Wealth and the Truly Good Life

Main Idea
The author of 1 Timothy describes the dangers of following false teachings in light of the true riches God gives and encourages believers to fight the good fight of faith. False teachers are motivated by greed, which generates from the worship of a false god. Rich Christians are called to "convert" from the false god of wealth to the true and living God.

Preparing to Lead
- Read and reflect on chapter 4, "Wealth and the Truly Good Life."
- Review this plan for the group gathering and select the questions and activities that you will use.
- What other questions, issues, or themes occur to you from your reflection?

Gathering
- Provide simple refreshments as people arrive and name tags if still needed.

Opening Worship
Prayer (unison)
O God, our life and our hope, we live in a world consumed by the desire to acquire more and more possessions. We confess that we have often been deceived by the empty promises of wealth. Let us rest in the confidence that you alone give life, and you give it abundantly. Teach us how to be grateful for what we have, generous with those who have not, and eager to receive from your hand the life that really is life. In the name of Christ, we pray. Amen.

Prayerful, Reflective Reading

- Read 1 Timothy 6:6–12 aloud.
- Invite all to reflect for a few minutes in silence.
- After reflection time, invite all to listen for a word or phrase as the passage is read again and to reflect on that word or phrase in silence.
- Read the passage a third time, asking all to offer a silent prayer following the reading.
- Invite volunteers to share the word or phrase that spoke most deeply to them.

Prayer

Loving God, hear our prayers today as we seek to follow you more faithfully:

(*spoken prayers may be offered*)

Hear us now as we pray together, saying, Our Father . . .

Conversation

- Introduce chapter 4, "Wealth and the Truly Good Life." Share observations, reflections, and insights.
- Review the Introduction (pp. 25–26). On a sheet of newsprint, write, "*What does the gospel have to say to the rich?*" Invite participants to share responses. Note the two other themes of 1 Timothy 6:3–19 and add these on the newsprint:

    The importance of sound teaching
    Fighting the good fight of faith

- Review "A Basic Theme: The Love of God versus the Love of Money" (pp. 26–28). Form several groups. Have the groups read 1 Timothy 6:3–10 and discuss the first question in For Reflection and Action (p. 30). Ask:

    What is the false teaching facing Timothy's congregation?

    Why is this false teaching so dangerous?

    Why is the love of God incompatible with the love of money?

- Review "The Life of Faith: Fighting the Good Fight" (pp. 28–29). Ask:

> *What does it mean (for Timothy and for us today) to "fight the good fight of the faith"?*
>
> *What does it mean to "take hold of the eternal life, to which you were called"?*

Spend a few minutes in quiet reflection on the statement: "The ultimate purpose of a Christian life is not to gain status, earn wealth, or accrue power, but to be a person of God and to do what one can to embody Christ's life in the world." Invite participants to write down one thing they can do—with God's help—to "embody Christ's life in the world."

- Review "The Church: Life in God Is True Riches" (pp. 29–30). Form several groups to discuss the quotes from *Rich Christians in an Age of Hunger* and the third question in For Reflection and Action (p. 31). Have each group share insights. Call attention to the question asked at the beginning of this group gathering: "*What does the gospel have to say to the rich?*" Ask:

> *Has your response to this question changed since reading and reflecting on 1 Timothy 6? If so, how?*
>
> *What does it mean for the rich to have "a conversion experience"?*

Conclusion

Invite participants to spend a moment remembering their baptisms, as suggested in For Reflection and Action (pp. 30–31). Read aloud 1 Timothy 6:17–19 as a closing charge (changing "they" language to "you," and so forth).

Passing the Peace

The peace of Christ be with you.
    And also with you.
Amen.

God's Word in Life, Story, and Scripture

Main Idea
The Pastor, speaking as Paul, tells the story of his own life, the story of Scripture, and the story of Timothy and his ministry. God's story and the human story become intertwined realities through our faith stories and the stories of contemporary "saints."

Preparing to Lead
- Read and reflect on chapter 5, "God's Word in Life, Story, and Scripture."
- Review this plan for the group gathering and select the questions and activities that you will use.
- What other questions, issues, or themes occur to you from your reflection?

Gathering
- Provide simple refreshments as people arrive and name tags if still needed.

Opening Worship
Prayer (unison)
O God, you are our life, and apart from you we can do nothing. Guide us through every valley of the shadow so that, at the end, we may confess that your strength and your love have enabled us to fight the good fight of faith and to finish the race. We pray this in the name of Jesus, who is the pioneer and the perfecter of our faith. Amen.

Prayerful, Reflective Reading

- Read 2 Timothy 3:10–4:8 aloud.
- Invite all to reflect for a few minutes in silence.
- After reflection time, invite all to listen for a word or phrase as the passage is read again and to reflect on that word or phrase in silence.
- Read the passage a third time, asking all to offer a silent prayer following the reading.
- Invite volunteers to share the word or phrase that spoke most deeply to them.

Prayer

Loving God, hear our prayers today as we seek to follow you more faithfully:

(*spoken prayers may be offered*)

Hear us now as we pray together, saying, Our Father . . .

Conversation

- Introduce chapter 5, "God's Word in Life, Story, and Scripture." Share observations, reflections, and insights.
- Review the Introduction (pp. 33–34). Read and compare the "signatures" in 1 Timothy 1:1, 2 Timothy 1:1, and Romans 1:1–6. Ask:

    What do these compressed narratives reveal about the writer's identity and story?

- Review "A Basic Theme: What You Have Seen in My Life" (pp. 34–35). On a sheet of newsprint, write "Paul's legacy." Have participants list the parts of Paul's legacy mentioned in 2 Timothy 3:10–13 (teaching, conduct, aim in life, faith, persecutions and suffering, and so forth). Discuss the first question in For Reflection and Action (p. 38). List on the newsprint examples of other Christians who have served as examples in the way they lived and/or suffered for the faith.
- Review "The Life of Faith: As for You, Timothy" (p. 36). Form several groups and discuss the second question in For Reflection and Action (p. 38). Also discuss:

How did the training Timothy received as a child prepare him for ministry as an adult?

How does Timothy's formation as a Christian compare to what you and/or your children have experienced in the church today?

• Review "The Church: As for Me" (pp. 37–38). On a sheet of newsprint, list the images Paul uses in 2 Timothy 4:6–8 to describe both death and the life of faith. Invite participants to reflect silently on the third question in For Reflection and Action (p. 38). Ask:

How do you like the words and images Paul uses to describe the life of faith? What would you express differently?

If you knew you were about to die, how would you sum up your life of faith?

Invite participants to share their thoughts with one or two others.

Conclusion
Invite participants to reflect daily on the third question in For Reflection and Action (p. 38).

Passing the Peace
The peace of Christ be with you.
    And also with you.
Amen.

The Endurance
of the Church

Main Idea

As in other New Testament letters, the small details at the ending of 2 Timothy—e.g., please bring my books and parchments—may seem random and miscellaneous at first. But they reveal a church moving ahead in confidence and mission, even in the face of adversity. They invite us to consider how the everyday actions of a church display its connection to the cosmic reality of Christ.

Preparing to Lead

- Read and reflect on chapter 6, "The Endurance of the Church."
- Review this plan for the group gathering and select the questions and activities that you will use.
- What other questions, issues, or themes occur to you from your reflection?

Gathering

- Provide simple refreshments as people arrive and name tags if still needed.

Opening Worship

Prayer (unison)

O God, we pray for your church. It has been the body of Christ throughout the generations. There have been many times when the church has not been faithful, but you have preserved and guided us by your grace. When the way before us is unclear, show us the right path, and when our feet hesitate because we cannot see where we are going, give us the light of your Word to steady our feet and to give us courage. In the name of the Lord of the church, Jesus Christ. Amen.

Prayerful, Reflective Reading

- Read 2 Timothy 4:9–22 aloud.
- Invite all to reflect for a few minutes in silence.
- After reflection time, invite all to listen for a word or phrase as the passage is read again and to reflect on that word or phrase in silence.
- Read the passage a third time, asking all to offer a silent prayer following the reading.
- Invite volunteers to share the word or phrase that spoke most deeply to them.

Prayer

Loving God, hear our prayers today as we seek to follow you more faithfully:

(*spoken prayers may be offered*)

Hear us now as we pray together, saying, Our Father . . .

Conversation

- Introduce chapter 6, "The Endurance of the Church." Share observations, reflections, and insights.
- Review the Introduction (pp. 39–40). Note that 2 Timothy ends, as do many letters and emails, with a number of small messages. Ask:

  Which of these small details do you find most interesting?

  What do they reveal about life in the early church?

  What similarities and differences do you see between the church of Paul and Timothy and faith communities today?

- Review "A Basic Theme: Working Together and Pulling Apart" (pp. 40–42). On a sheet of newsprint, list all the people named in 2 Timothy 4:9–22. Note that the names reveal a church that is like a family but also a cosmic reality—spread around the world. Form several groups and discuss the first question in For Reflection and Action (p. 45).

- Review "The Life of Faith: The Frailty of Humans and the Faithfulness of God" (pp. 42–43). Form two groups to look more closely at 2 Timothy 4:9–22. Have one group look for examples of human frailties causing problems in the church. Have the other group look for evidence of God's faithfulness. Invite the groups to share their lists. Have participants reflect silently on the second question in For Reflection and Action (p. 45). Then have them pair up and share their thoughts.
- Review "The Church: Useful Christians, Risk-Taking Christians" (pp. 43–44). Share these key points:
  a. Mark is used as an example of a "useful" Christian—useful in the sense of providing Paul with the things he needs.
  b. The metaphor of household utensils in 2 Timothy 2:20–21 suggests another meaning of "useful"—doing the holy work of Christ in and through the church.
  c. Prisca and Aquila are examples of "risk takers." In Romans 16:4, we learn that they "risked their necks" for Paul.

Discuss the third question in For Reflection and Action (p. 45). On a sheet of newsprint, write "Useful," "Risk Takers," and any other types of Christians mentioned by participants. Ask:

Why are each of these important in the church?

Which type are you?

Conclusion
Read 2 Timothy 4:22 as a benediction.

Passing the Peace
The peace of Christ be with you.
    And also with you.
Amen.

Glossary*

baptism. The incorporation of believers into Jesus Christ by faith. Baptism gathers up one's life and ordains all believers to a holy vocation in Christ.

bishop. Elders in a cluster of house churches in a region or large town in early churches had an overseer called a bishop (Greek, *episcopos*).

deacons. Those who led early churches in the practical work of caring for widows and others in need (Greek, *diakonos*).

doctrine. Church teachings of Christian beliefs. In the early church they functioned as expressions of wisdom that opened up ways of seeing, trusting, and living.

elder. Leader of house churches in early churches (Greek, *presbyteros*).

faith. Belief in church teachings but also deep trust in Jesus Christ.

gospel. The good news of Jesus Christ. In the early church, the gospel became a fairly settled body of teachings.

kingdom of God. The reign of God in Jesus Christ in which Christ is Lord of all and Lord now in the lives and hearts of Christian believers.

Pastoral Epistles. The three New Testament letters of 1 and 2 Timothy and Titus.

prayer. People speak and listen to God in prayer. This takes place in the context of a deep and trusting relationship with God.

worship. The ritual focus of the Christian life in expressions of praise and thanksgiving to God. A worship service is a long conversation between God and worshipers through Scripture and sermon. People speak to God through prayers, creeds, hymns, and ascriptions of praise. Worship is a dialogue between God and people, a sign that the whole of worship is prayer.

---

* The definitions here relate to ways these terms are used in this study. Further study can be made in other resources such as Donald K. McKim, *The Westminster Dictionary of Theological Terms*, 2nd ed. (Louisville, KY: Westminster John Knox Press, 2014).

Want to Know More?

Bassler, Jouette M. *1 Timothy, 2 Timothy, Titus*. Nashville: Abingdon Press, 1996.

Donelson, Lewis R. *Colossians, Ephesians, First and Second Timothy, and Titus*. Westminster Bible Companion. Louisville, KY: Westminster John Knox Press, 1996.

Long, Thomas G. *1 and 2 Timothy and Titus*. Belief: A Theological Commentary on the Bible. Louisville, KY: Westminster John Knox Press, 2016.

Oden, Thomas C. *First and Second Timothy and Titus*. Interpretation: A Bible Commentary for Teaching and Preaching. Louisville, KY: John Knox Press, 2012.

Wright, Tom. *Paul for Everyone: the Pastoral Letters : 1 and 2 Timothy and Titus*. Louisville, KY: Westminster John Knox Press, 2004.